# This Cats' Eye View book belongs to

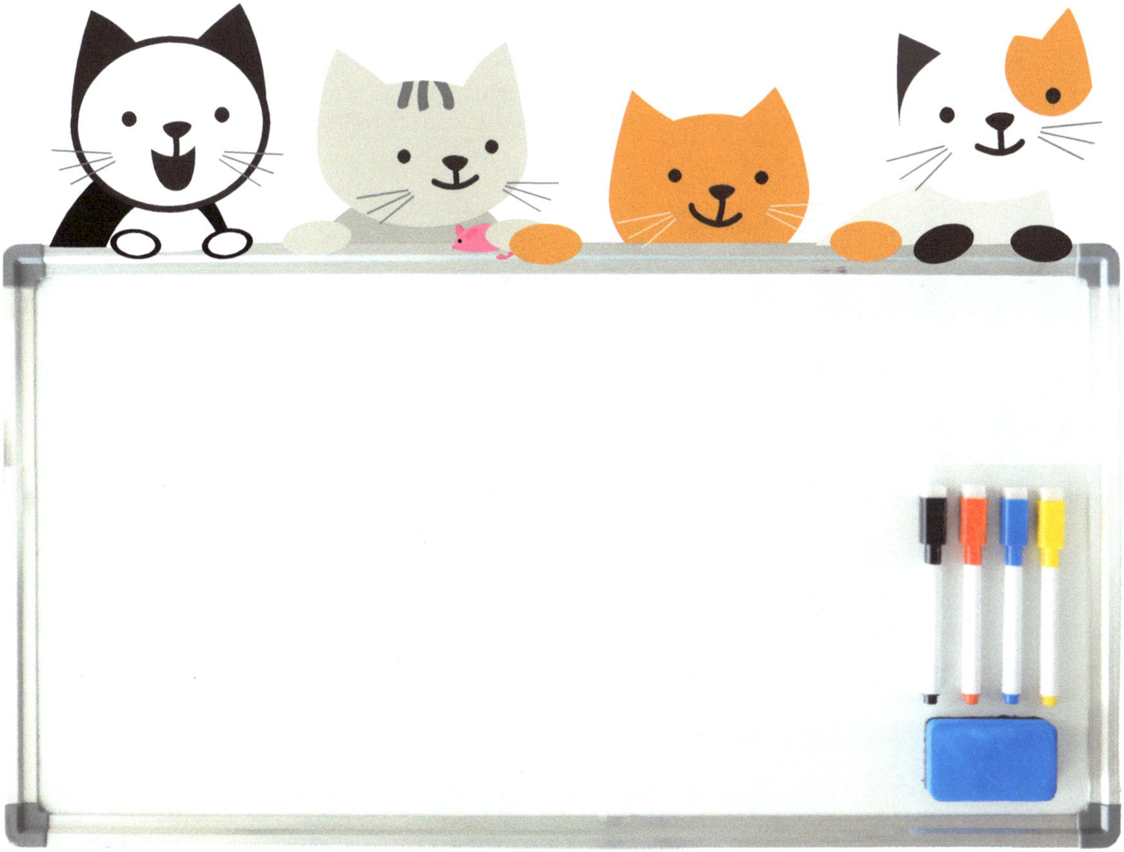

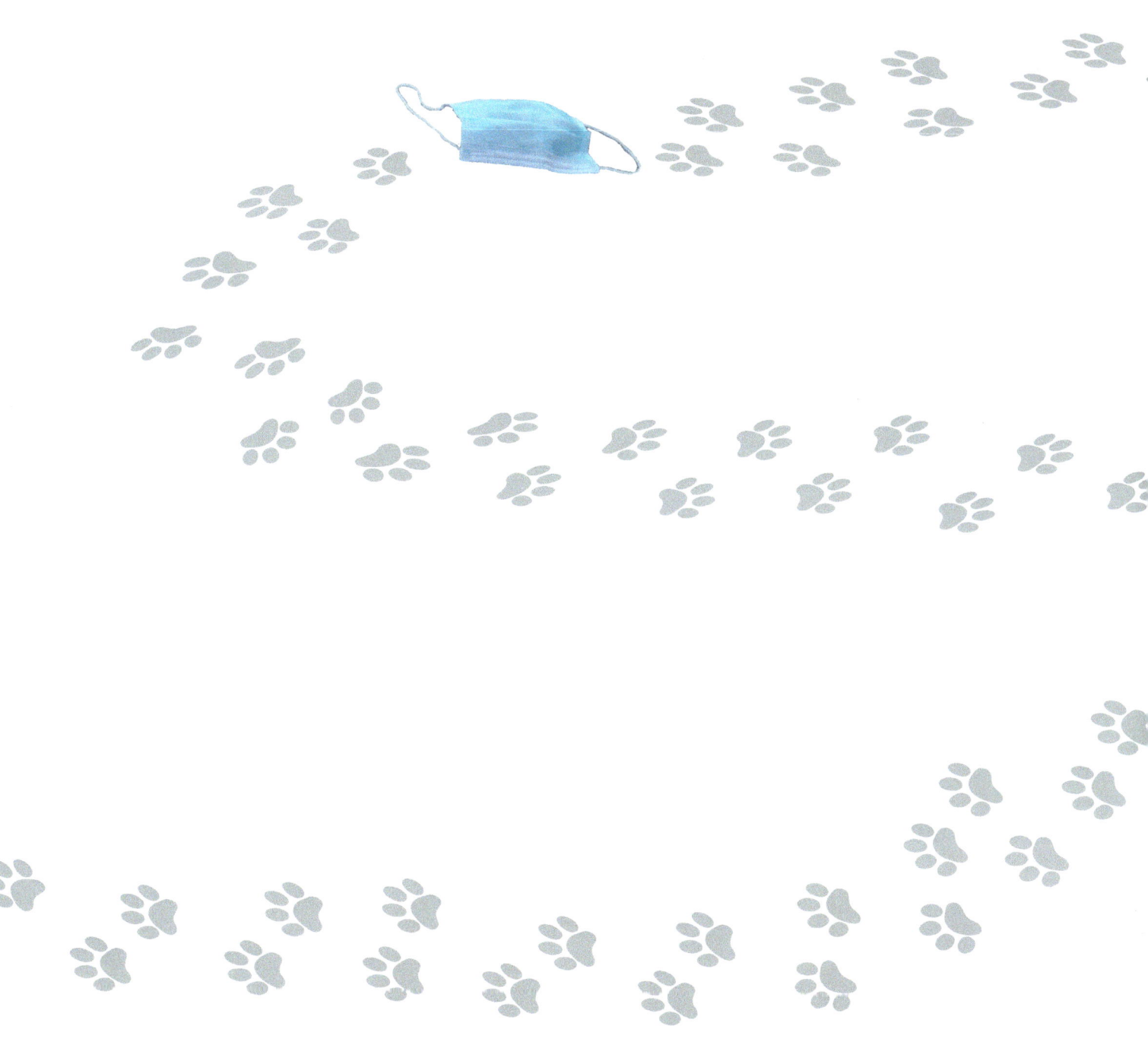

# Dedicated to our girls

Special thanks to:

My wonderful editor Tonie Lambie,

Copyright © 2022 Octavia Lonergan.

All rights reserved. This book or any portion thereof may not be reproduced or used in any manner whatsoever without the express written permission of the author except for the use of brief quotations in a book review.

# Cats' Eye View of LITTER

Written & illustrated by Octaviu Lonergan

Tibby strolls along the wall carrying her **mouse**.

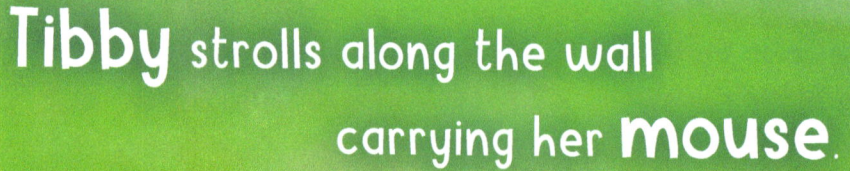

When there's too much **noise** inside, she likes to **leave the house**.

Glancing down across the **lawn** her **friends** come into view —

Ozzy's stretched out on the grass,
Leo, and Mimi too!

Something's **bothering** her today
and so she feels she **needs a chat.**

If you need some **wise advice...**
the one to ask -
another **cat!**

" Sometimes when it's **nearly dark**
I like to roam around the **park**.

Yesterday, I must confess
the park was in
**a dreadful mess!** "

Who else do you think could have caused the mess?

But I asked them

(from a distance)

**not them**, they said, with firm insistence."

Bins were full up - **overflowing** -
**rubbish** humans had been throwing.

Strewn around across the grass
were **plastic** bottles,
**food** and **glass**.

"Their rubbish could cause **harm** to others – fathers, mothers, sisters, brothers.

They really should **take home their waste** and if they don't, they're a **disgrace!**"

Nodding **wisely**, **Ozzy** speaks,
the oldest of the four.

The others all look up to him,
his words have **helped** before.

" It happens at the **beaches**, too.
Well, that's what I have heard.

The **litter** could **hurt** anyone:
A child, a pet, a bird! "

Little **creatures** could get **trapped** in **rubbish** on the ground. Stuck inside a **bag** or **tin** -

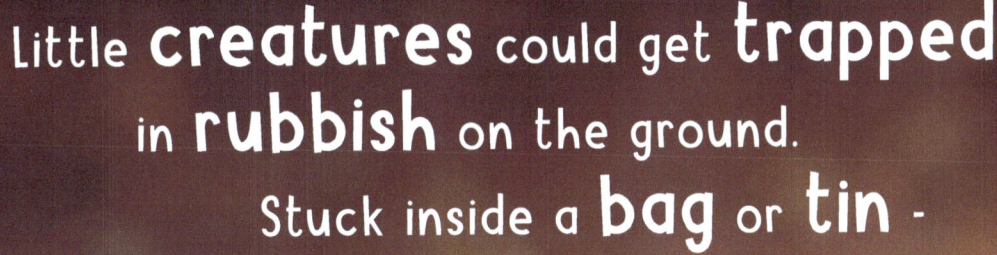

who knows when they'd be **found?**

What other animals might get hurt by litter, and how?

It's also **bad** for **planet Earth**...
It's quite hard to explain.
But I will try, for what it's worth,
to make it **clear** and **plain**.

The **damage** can go deeper than the ground on which it's thrown, **polluting soil** and **water** too,

as sometimes it gets blown away across the grass into a nearby **lake** or **pond**.

Or from the **shore**

into the **sea**,

then drifting far beyond.

What is happening to
the turtle above?

# About the Author

Octavia's love of writing poems stretches back to childhood, along with a passion for creating art and music. In 2020 she finally realised her dream of becoming a children's author.

Also a graphic designer with over 20 years' professional experience, Octavia lives in Surrey, England with her husband, and their twin daughters - her inspiration and motivation.

Learn more at poemsbyoctavia.com

If you've enjoyed this book, please do leave a review!
Just scan the QR code below.

Next in the series...

# Cats' Eye View of Being Green

To keep up-to-date follow
@poemsbyoctavia on social media

www.ingramcontent.com/pod-product-compliance
Lightning Source LLC
Chambersburg PA
CBHW040022130526
44590CB00036B/66